MW01287070

Appalachia
Boy
A Memoir

By Dr. George Lucas

Dedicated

to the women in my life

First and foremost, my wife, *Eleanor Sudol Lucas, who has has guided and supported me for the past 50 years*

My mother: *Anna Forni Lucas*

My sister: *Margaret Jean Lucas Schmidt*

My grandmothers: *Mollie Workman Forni and Alda Lucas Okey*

My aunts: *Lottie Forni, Alberta Forni Brock, Dena Forni Cook, and Anne Okey Pendelton*

My daughters: *Diane Greer Lucas, Ashley Gayle Lucas, and Whitney Lucas Rosenberg*

My granddaughters: *Corrine Gilbert Lucas, Abigail Gilbert Lucas, Hadley Chance Rosenberg, Sophia Arisbe DeWaal, and Chloe Eleanor Lucas*

Appalachia Boy: A Memoir
was edited and designed by Brian Whepley, a writer, editor, and designer in Wichita, Kansas (bwcommunicates.com)

Copyright © 2017
George Lucas
1715 N. Cypress,
Wichita, KS 67206
316-634-0585
ISBN 978-0-692-85729-8

Off to a Poor Start

DYLAN THOMAS suggested in *Under Milk Wood* that we should begin at the beginning. Makes sense.

My mother once said that the Depression came and went and we never knew the difference. We were poor when it started and poor when it was over. Of course we were poor. We're from Appalachia.

The Appalachian Mountain Range extends from Quebec and Newfoundland to Alabama. Geographically, Appalachia includes all of West Virginia and certain counties of Kentucky, Ohio, Maryland, Tennessee, North Carolina, Virginia and Georgia. The population of the central and southern highlands of this ancient mountain range is frequently thought of as comprising a distinct sociocultural region known as "Appalachia." Many members of this population are, and were, non-commercial, semi-self-sufficient farmers. Gradually, a stereotype formed of an image of a society that held with much of its 18th century heritage. People were thought of as noble and savage, independent, proud, rugged and violent but also as dirty and uneducated yet crafty and practical. They drank too much and were lazy but managed to produce excessively large families. This is probably enough background to situate Somerton, Ohio, in one of the poorest parts of the United States. Somerton was originally named Somerset but when another Somerset was discovered in Ohio, the name of Somerset was given to the township and the town's name became Somerton. The town is a bit like Dylan Thomas wrote in *Under Milk Wood* when he described his hometown in Wales as inhabited by a few hundred self-satisfied people living along a single street where nothing much ever happened.

After the Civil War Northerners came into contact with the Southern mountains and were surprised to find mineral and timber wealth coupled with a romantic beauty. Unfortunately, much of that beauty has been destroyed in the 20th century by the primary resource — coal. Strip mining has carved off the mountaintops and left ugly scars on the land. Despite the general prosperity in America, the 1950's were a time of extreme poverty in Appalachia and Lyndon Johnson's "War on Poverty" generally failed in Appalachia. I suspect part of the reason for this is the general distrust of outsiders and the inhabitants' stubborn individuality. As you might imagine, 1952 was not a great time to graduate from high school in Barnesville, Ohio. Barnesville is a neighboring town eight miles up a winding road where we were sent after our local school in Somerton was closed down and, of course, when the school closes the town deteriorates further. Somerton still exists, after a fashion, and on September 9, 2015, celebrated, modestly I suspect, its 200th year of existence as a town.

Small-town Obstetrics

"**Rome, if she yells or screams**, put this chloroform-soaked gauze over her nose for a couple of breaths. Mrs. Gibbons and I will take care of the birthing if you will tend to the anesthesia," said Doc Reeder as he looked at my mother moaning in the family bed crammed into the small bedroom of a tiny house in Somerton on October 3, 1934. Thus, I came into this world, with my auto mechanic father at the head of the bed and a midwife and a family doctor orchestrating the affair. People seem obsessed with knowing the weight and length of a newborn. I don't know where I was

The author, George Lucas, at 2.

on those scales but apparently I was a keeper. I wonder what my father was thinking as the young family expanded by one a little over a year after he and my mother were married. The details of my father's previous marriage and subsequent divorce were never discussed as far as I know but I'm sure a 10-year age difference was a concern at least to my grandmother and Mother's sisters, especially Lottie, the spinster schoolteacher.

I wonder also if Daddy's hands were clean for such an event. I'm certain they were not. He was a mechanic after all, and as hard as he tried scrubbing the grime away with Lava soap, there were still lines of black grease in the creases of his skin and under the fingernails. Daddy's hands were not graceful either, but although strong and sturdy they were capable of great tenderness when he hugged or caressed us children. Ultimately there were four of us, although my youngest brother Duane didn't arrive until a month after Daddy died in January 1945. I'm certain he loved us, as he liked to roughhouse with us and tease us and he particularly liked to grab us when he had a day or two's growth of chin whiskers and "beard" us. He occasionally administered some physical punishment with a switch or a razor strop, but I'm sure we deserved every licking we got. Frequently, just going out back into the yard with the threat of cutting off a switch would produce a confession and a promise of better behavior. He was of average height, balding, with a "Hitler type" black mustache. He was lightly educated, having given up formal schooling after just one day of high school. I never saw him read a book, although he did read the newspaper occasionally. He was fun-loving and gregarious as opposed to my mother, who had some college education and was a thin, very serious woman who gradually morphed into a relentless depression in later life. She was stoic enough that she apparently never seriously considered remarrying after Daddy died, although a local farmer expressed some interest in her but we vetoed the idea when she called all of the children together to ask if we thought she should marry Mansel Hagan! So much for family consultations, and she remained a widow the remainder of her life.

Rabbits and Gunshot Wounds

SINCE I HAVE BEEN DOCTORING for most of my life, perhaps this story should really begin with a doctor, albeit a different one. 1939 was not a good time to be graduating from medical school, and there were not many opportunities for a man with a new black bag and a barely used stethoscope to begin a practice. So it was that Paul Johnson, MD, landed in the tiny village of Somerton in southeastern Ohio. Somerton was one of two small towns in Somerset Township, and it was really a village although there were three general stores, two filling stations, a feed store, a hardware store and a funeral parlor to serve the 200 white, Anglo-Saxon inhabitants and the surrounding farmers who worked small, subsistence dairy farms. Oh yes, there were two churches — Methodist and the Church of Christ — and members of each considered members of the other heathens, although both groups were rather pious when contrasted to the drinkin', gamblin' Catholics who lived in an even smaller village deep in the holler at the far end of the township. The name of that burg was Temperanceville, an anomaly of nomenclature if there ever was one! Temperanceville did have a barbershop where you could get a haircut and listen to a lot of dirty jokes for 25 cents, but most people went to Temperanceville for the readily available home brew and moonshine. Temperanceville was another one-street town, and the first house one encountered as one entered the burg was the conveniently located bootlegger's operation.

But, back to Doc Johnson. In fact, I'm not at all sure his first name was Paul as everyone called him "Doc." Doc apparently couldn't find work anywhere else so he dropped into Somerton in the summer of 1939 and set up shop. He and his wife drove up in a small sort of camping trailer and parked it in the vacant lot behind Fatty Warton's house, opened up an awning in front of the trailer and literally hung out a shingle as a general practitioner. I am assuming that Mr. Warton charged him rent for the use of his lot, but then again Mr. Warton, being one of the major figures of the town (he owned one of the grocery stores and garage), may have seen bringing a doctor to town as a civic duty. This sort of an outdoor office worked quite well as long as it didn't rain and, of course, would serve only for the duration of the summer.

Somerton is a one-street town through which coursed Ohio Route 8. The town started on top of a hill, leveled off in the center and then started another downhill slope at the lower two-thirds of the town. The town gave way to long parallel valleys, almost ravines, on either side of the road behind the single row of houses and outbuildings. Doc Johnson's "office" was conveniently located in the center, flat part of the town, although to get to Fatty's back lot required a fairly steep descent from the road. I mention these topographical features as they figure into the first time I met Doc Johnson.

We lived near the top of the hill on the "North Slope" in a house my father had put together from the remains of a long-defunct creamery. When I was 5 years old, I wandered onto the road, where I was hit by a high school kid careering down the hill on his bicycle. The impact knocked me back into the front yard with multiple scrapes, abrasions and bruises. I don't remember what damage was done to the bicycle or the cyclist, but my mother whisked me down to the new doctor's office, where an examination showed I had no broken bones. The abrasions were cleansed and covered with bandages and varicolored adhesive tape, and I was sent on my merry way. I didn't quite learn the lesson about crossing the street, as I had a more frightening encounter with a car a couple years later. I'll skip the details but suffice it to say I probably wasn't as scared as the spinster schoolteacher who was driving the car! Fortunately, my first meeting with a moving vehicle was with a bike and not a car, otherwise I probably wouldn't have any kind of story to tell.

Doc later moved his office to a small building on the "South" side of town before winter set in, and he and his wife and daughter were able to buy a small house a couple doors up the street from the office. Our family had a number of encounters with Doc for a variety of ailments but probably the one I remember most vividly has to do with a gunshot wound — self-inflicted. When I was 9 years old, my father thought I was old enough to handle a gun and allowed me to use a .22 rifle and began to take me on rabbit or squirrel hunting expeditions. Probably the fondest memories I have of my father were those of going hunting in the fall as well as fishing in the summer. I was also allowed to use the gun to shoot at birds, tin cans and such, and I remember one time my grandfather, who was a bird and animal lover, being especially angry with me for shooting a bird. I didn't think it was such a bad thing — after all, it was only a cat bird! To my knowledge I didn't kill any livestock on adjacent farms or deplete the population of Somerton with stray bullets, but the rifle did have one bad feature. It had a "hair trigger," meaning that it took not much more than a puff of wind to discharge it. Daddy tried to fix it a couple times but never very successfully, and he always warned me to be careful that I didn't touch the trigger till I was ready to fire.

One fall day in 1944, my pal Jim Mahoney and I went down into an adjacent hollow — holler in the local vernacular — to hunt rabbits. He had a .410 shotgun and I my "trusty" rifle. It was a cold day and I remember having on a pair of canvas gloves as well as a jacket and stocking cap. There were even a few patches of snow remaining from an earlier snowfall, which we thought might make finding a rabbit easier. We tramped around for a while looking for the elusive hare when we spied what we took for a rabbit's hole in the ground. While I was peering into the hole, my rifle went off and I suddenly realized that my glove had been blown off my left hand and there was an area of numbness around a small hole (it looked quite large actually) in my middle finger, which was rapidly becoming painful. Apparently the gun, which I'd had in my right hand, had brushed against an adjacent bush and discharged. Jim realized I'd been shot and we began to walk back to town, but the more Jim realized we were likely to be in trouble for this accident, the less he was interested in helping me back home. He decided he was going to keep hunting and delay facing the music from his parents saying, "I'll see ya," and headed back down the holler. By this time the finger was throbbing something awful and each step of the half mile or so I had to walk to get back to the house seemed to jar the hand more so that by the time I reached the back porch of our house I was feeling mighty weak and mighty sick. It hurt too much to open the door, so I simply kicked on the back door and yelled for my Mother, who answered the door to find a pale and frightened 10-year-old. Probably when I called out that I had shot myself prepared her for the worst. She quickly called my father, who was working in his garage — Daddy was a mechanic who operated an independent gas station and car repair shop next door. When told what had happened, he said, "I knew that damn boy was going to shoot himself one day."

He bundled me up in the car and we drove the quarter of a mile to Doc Johnson's office. Doc took a look at my middle finger, blackened from powder burns with a hole on the palm side (entry) and the back of the finger (exit), dissolved some sulfa powder in a beaker of water (probably it was saline) and plopped my throbbing hand into the beaker. This was 1944 and sulfa had just become available for civilian use after years of successful use of the drug on the battlefield, and I think Doc felt it would cure most anything. Anyway, after a few minutes soaking, he got out a sterile probe and ran it through my finger a few times — I'm glad

I don't remember how much that hurt — dumped more sulfa powder into the wound and dressed it and advised Daddy to bring me back the next day. He also gave us an envelope full of large, white sulfa pills for me to take by mouth. Needless to say, over the next week or 10 days I got a lot of sulfa and why my kidneys still work is a mystery. Doc knew that the thing to do was to keep the wound open and that he did, daily or every other day, with his damn sterile probe. I must say the finger works well now with only a little numbness that I barely notice unless I bump the right spot on the bottom of the finger. After we had finished up at the doctor's that first day, Daddy decided that it was too late to get anything done in the garage so we went three miles down the road to the nearest tavern so he could fortify himself from the awful experience he'd just had. I don't recall whether I went into the Corner Grill or waited in the car that time or not, but I was in there many times in later years as Somerton was a dry area and many a resident of Somerton made the three-mile trip to "Malagee" every evening to refresh themselves. The town was actually named Malaga, having nothing whatsoever to do with the Spanish city of that name, and, if you can believe it, was even smaller than Somerton.

Doc Johnson, fat and rotund, was the sort of a guy everyone felt comfortable with. He didn't put on airs, although his wife could be a bit snooty, and he was simply a member of our community. He was short, overweight and "told it like it was," occasionally telling people they were too fat or too thin or drank too much. One popular legend was that he said to a lady, "Ruth, I don't know what's the matter with you, but you're sure in a helluva shape!" He was very kind to us and I doubt that he ever sent my mother a bill for seeing one of us after my father died. He was equally kind to others as well and graciously accepted a chicken, a dozen fresh eggs or some summer sausage as payment for an office visit. As I ventured into the medical field I often thought back to Doc Johnson. His generosity and his straightforward way of dealing with patients honestly and fairly made an impression on me.

A Profound Death

THE DEATH OF MY FATHER, Rome Lamoyne Lucas, on January 3, 1945, had a profound effect on my mother, brothers, sister and me. This event also relates to Doc Johnson, for Daddy was out playing cards with Doc and some other men the evening of New Year's Day. Mom and the other wives apparently sat home and listened to the radio or, more likely, simply went to bed early. At any rate my father came home quite early in the morning of January 2 and later in the morning complained of a headache, which my mother attributed to a hangover. I'm sure she wasn't too sympathetic. After he lay down on the living room couch, he fell asleep and after a couple hours Mom thought he should get up. Despite her urgings and pleadings, "Rome, it's time to get up," he couldn't be aroused. After trying to awaken him for a while, she realized that something was wrong and called Doc Johnson. Doc came up to the house and to no avail tried some things to awaken Daddy and, suspecting I don't know what, said he would have to be taken to Wheeling, West Virginia, to a hospital. Harold Steele, the undertaker and town savant who lived half a dozen houses down the street in the funeral home, came up and they bundled Daddy into the hearse and set off for Wheeling. The weather that January day was cold and snowy, and they told my mother that they were going to drive very carefully for fear of sliding off the road and allowing Daddy to freeze to death! We children were trundled off to Barnesville for my Grandmother and Grandfather Forni to take care of us during this crisis. For some reason Mother stayed at home, although I'm sure someone must have been concerned that she might go into early labor — she was pregnant with Duane, my youngest brother. I was 10 years old at the time, my sister Margaret Jean — in the pseudo South of southeastern Ohio all girls used two names — was 8, my brother David was 6 and Duane had not arrived yet. We were all sitting in my grandmother's living room waiting for word of what was happening when the phone rang on January 3 and Grandma answered, listened for a moment and said, "Oh, you poor children." Daddy had died without ever waking up, leaving my mother a widow with three small children and a fourth in her

Rome Lamoyne Lucas with Hotshot.

belly who would not arrive for another five weeks. Mom seemed to accept all this rather stoically. The only time anyone saw her weep was when she was informed that there was no doctor waiting at the Wheeling hospital when Daddy was admitted. To my knowledge, no antemortem diagnosis was ever made and no effective treatment instituted. In retrospect, what killed him was a subdural hematoma, a blood clot between the brain and the skull, which is rather easily diagnosed and easily treated by a fairly simple neurosurgical operation nowadays. An autopsy was performed that established the diagnosis. I remember a couple days later noticing a piece of gauze sticking out from behind Daddy's head as it lay on the satin pillow of the coffin, a souvenir of the autopsy table!

In the few weeks after my father died, it became known that Daddy had bumped his head while working under a truck at his job at the M & K grocery distributors. He mentioned the bump on his head to a neighbor to whom he had given a ride home and she, after learning the details of my father's death, volunteered the information. A blow on the head is the exact clinical scenario that leads to a subdural hematoma days or even weeks after the incident. Armed with the knowledge of a work-related injury, my mother filed for death benefits with the help of a lawyer. I think it took three or four years before the case got settled and my mother received $5,000, a goodly portion of which went to the barrister.

The next few days were a bit of a blur with lots of neighbors and relatives coming by — Father had four half brothers and one half sister, each of whom had several children, while Mother had three sisters and two brothers with a few children of their own. Of course, in a small town everyone acts like relatives and they drop in willy-nilly. Daddy attended church only under duress, perhaps at Christmas or Easter, so the funeral was held in the funeral home rather than in the Methodist church. Aside from the muffled voices, the sobbing and the smell of flowers, I don't remember much about the service except that Mother had selected Tennyson's "Crossing the Bar" to be read: "Sunset and Evening Star, And one clear call for me! And may there be no moaning of the bar, when I put out to sea."

After the service there was the short trip to the Barnesville cemetery on that cold January day and, after a few more prayers I suppose, Harold Steele said, "You all go on home now. We'll take care of Rome." The other thing that sticks out in my mind was the following Christmas when all the relatives came bearing gifts. We never had such a bountiful Christmas in our little house, but by the next year we were essentially forgotten. Various relatives

David, Margaret Jean, George and Duane Lucas.

dropped by from time to time and Uncle Robert and Aunt Libby apparently sent Mother a check periodically over the next several years. I do carry one legacy from Daddy — my middle name. Lamoyne translates from the French as, "the monk." Where my grandmother found that name and tagged Father with it, I have no idea.

Squirrel Hunting

As I sit on my back porch smoking a cigar some 70 years later, recalling my use of the dangerous .22 rifle and the events of 1944, I'm reminded of the times my father took me squirrel hunting. Today, I enjoy watching the squirrels in my backyard gambol up the trunk of the cypress tree or scamper along the stone wall that my neighbor put up when he built his house. The squirrel runs up and down the branches, occasionally stopping to nibble on the new leaves on the tree. The squirrel is often joined by his, or her, cousin and they chase each other around the branches. This frenetic activity is contrasted with the mournful calling of a dove perched on the rooftop of a nearby house, and occasionally they are joined by the hooting of an owl sitting on a chimney. These squirrels all seem to be of the red or "fox squirrel" variety living in an urban environment. They behave a bit differently than those living in the woods around Somerton, many of whom were the smaller grey squirrels. A good deal of stealth is required to successfully shoot one of the wilder ones. That, of course, is what Dad and I were trying to do. Once the walk to the woods was complete and we had reached a place that he had staked out, squirrel hunting was not very strenuous. Daddy would occasionally lean back against a tree and take a nap while admonishing us to keep our eyes and ears open for the wily rodent. I suspect that a nip from the jug of wine he kept in the trunk of the car helped with his restfulness. We were not always successful but being out in the woods on a fall day with a bit of a nip in the air, with no noise except for the rustle of the leaves, the occasional chatter of a squirrel or a bird chirping in the trees or the distant barking of a dog, remains an unforgettable experience. Additionally, braised squirrel is rather tasty, but not as good as rabbit stew, particularly if you don't bite down on a piece of buckshot.

Sensations

I LIKE FLOWERS and the scent of flowers, just as I like perfume and men's cologne. Many of these scents are evocative of people, places or things, but there is one compound scent that always reminds me of my visit to see Minor Reed. I was taken to see Mr. Reed by my mother and grandmother when I was about 5 years old. He was a cousin of my grandmother's, who, incidentally, had an evocative smell of her own. Mr. Reed lived in a large white house at the corner of Wiley Avenue and North Street a couple of houses from Grandmother's. For the next 20 years I always took note of that corner house when I visited Grandmother Forni. Reed didn't have much to say at the time of our visit. You see, he was dead and this was really a visitation. I still remember the dim lights, the pinkish light bulbs, the flowers and the casket where Mr. Reed, dressed in a brown suit, had been "laid out" in the living room. Most of all I remember the smell of the assembled flowers. The smell never seems to change, and it was certainly noticeable when my father lay in repose at Steele's funeral home. I assume it's the combination of lilies, roses and carnations, but every time I have to go to a funeral parlor or a funeral, I'm transported to that long-ago time of Minor Reed's wake.

Harold Steele, the undertaker, lived at the funeral home a couple of houses down the street from us. He also owned a larger house next door where he stored coffins and other tools of his trade. The house was a large three-story structure, most of which, except for the closed-off coffin room, was rented out to

Jim Mahoney's family. The Mahoney family consisted of the father, Steward, who always seemed to have a pipe in his mouth and who supported the family by working in a tire recapping garage, Mother Hazel, Janice, Susan, Mary Lou, Sharon, Jim and a younger brother, Neil, who was a diabetic and not very robust. Jim and I were the same age and grew up together, and his Aunt Lela was our third- and fourth-grade teacher. Although the coffin storage part of the house was closed off and dark, Jim would occasionally figure a way to unlock the door and would entertain some of the rest of us to a tour of the spooky place. We were quite fascinated by the partially emptied bottles of pink embalming fluid we found in the funeral home's trash. There was no such thing as garbage collection in our little town, and every house had a small trash heap out back. There was a larger community trash heap south of town that was a great place to rummage, and we found all sorts of things we thought might be useful. Also a great place to get cut on the broken glass or get a nail in your foot.

We spent a lot of time out doors — running around, foraging in the trash heaps as well as two or three abandoned, or at least unoccupied, houses. We never got caught in these trespassing episodes but the time we found some dynamite caps in an old shed could have ended in some tragic publicity. For some reason, I wanted to see what the dynamite cap was made of and in trying to get it open tried to open it with my teeth. Fortunately, it was a dud or I might have had my head blown off! Just by being outside we learned a lot about animals and plants, as well as the birds and the bees. We recognized birdcalls, the bark of different dogs or foxes and, of course, which plants were poisonous or toxic. Hunting small game and fishing in the local creeks or ponds took up a fair bit of our time as well. Seining a shallow creek for fish bait was always interesting as we usually netted a snake or two. They were not pleased, hissing and opening their fearsome mouths. The prize was some small creatures called hellgrammites that made excellent fish bait. A more common and easy source of fish bait was the night crawlers that showed up at night when it rained. A flashlight and a quick hand plus a coffee can with a bunch of grass for storage were all that was required. We also learned which type of leaves could be dried and smoked. One of our better sources of tobacco was the cigarette butts we picked up along the side of the road. Yuk! But I guess that was no more dangerous than diving into shallow creeks or climbing to the top of large trees. I learned to swim without benefit of lessons but simply went to the creek with the other boys where we taught ourselves to swim among the turtles and the snakes who didn't appreciate our intrusions We did get a bit of formal instruction in baseball and basketball when we got to high school but otherwise we learned as we went along. We seemed to make whatever adjustments in terms of choosing up sides to play ball were necessary and didn't fight too much. This does remind me of the time my friend Dick Detling got a pair of boxing gloves, so we tried that a couple of times. Getting hit in the nose didn't appeal to me so that part of my manly development got omitted fairly quickly.

Working to Put Bread on the Table

OUR LIVES CHANGED considerably after Daddy died. Our family was never well off even when we had a breadwinner, but we certainly dropped below the poverty line in January of 1945. I'm not so sure that the term "poverty line" had been coined at that time, but we definitely qualified as poor. There were some safety nets including Social Security payment to widows and surviving children and local county programs that allowed us to get medical and dental care, i.e. welfare. Another county benefit very important to a young boy who loved to read was the bookmobile, which paid Somerton a visit once a month when weather permitted. The big green van parked in front of the former bank building, and we would go and select a few books from the shelves of this small library, which were surprisingly abundant. With the return of the bookmobile a month later, the books would be replaced with new selections. Books about travel and adventure were especially sought, such as *Robinson Crusoe*, *The Swiss Family Robinson*, Richard Halliburton's tale of swimming the Hellespont and *All Quiet on the Western Front*.

In the weeks following my father's death my mother struggled through the final weeks of her fourth pregnancy. In February, my mother delivered, with Doc Johnson attending, a healthy boy in the same bed at home where the rest of us had been born. Doc was assisted by his daughter, a registered nurse. In anticipation of the birth, the bed had been moved downstairs, replacing the table in the small dining room at the back of the house. Since the assistance of neighbors and relatives tapered in the months after Daddy died, Mother decided she would have to go to work, and took a couple of us along with her. She became the janitor of the Methodist church across the street, and three of us kids worked with her to keep the place clean. We were responsible for ringing the church bell on Sunday mornings. We had no choice but to stay for Sunday school and services.

Mother also became the janitor for the four-room elementary school, a job she couldn't possibly have done without our help. The school functioned with two grades in each of the four rooms. Despite a large number of kids under the supervision of a single teacher, it wasn't too chaotic, due largely, I suspect, to necessary physical and verbal abuse. Fortunately, there were no toilets to clean, as the toilets were two wooden four-holers down behind the school. If you discounted the smell, they could be considered to more or less clean themselves with the help of a sprinkling of lime. The school was heated with coal, with a large stove in the back of each room stoked periodically by the teacher from a pile in the coal bin. My job was to fill the coal bins each evening, carrying buckets of dirty, dusty bituminous coal from the coal shed behind the school. Those buckets were heavy, and many trips were required to fill four coal bins every evening, as I was a puny 10-year-old. When I blew my nose after I got home, I would get a handkerchief full of black snot! I also was responsible for the furnace at the Methodist church, but all I had to do there was shovel coal into the furnace with no carrying involved. I also acquired a paper route delivering the Martin's Ferry *Times Leader* every evening during the week. I learned a lot from that experience — people who complained that their paper was late or wet, and the cheapskates who tried to get out of paying up for the paper when I came around to collect once a month. The paper wasn't worth much; perhaps I got a half-cent a paper. Despite the cheapskates, there were customers on the other side of the divide who would give me a couple extra dollars at Christmas time. The paper route had another benefit in terms of my physical fitness.

Appalachia Boy

Running up and down the hills of the town was definitely a good thing. Since the paper had to be delivered every day except Sunday, I think it taught me something about reliability.

Sometime after my father died, the Social Security payments to widows and dependent children kicked in — the princely sum of $18.00 a month per child certainly wasn't enough to sustain a family of five, and the janitor jobs didn't add much to the coffers either. When Duane was about 10 months old, he was left with a neighbor who baby-sat him, and Mom took a job as a teacher in a one-room school — all eight grades. She had gone to school at Muskingum College long enough to get a teaching certificate but had given up teaching to marry my father. This school was six or seven miles away, so Mother either took the bus that ran between Barnesville and Woodsfield through Somerton or bummed a ride off someone who was going that way. Mother always claimed she was too nervous to drive and after Daddy died she sold the old Plymouth. Teaching school under those conditions didn't help her "nervousness" much either, and she began a lifelong struggle with depression. Who wouldn't be depressed! I suspect the stress of raising four kids as a widow with limited income contributed to the development of rheumatoid arthritis that ravaged her body over the next 40 years. Subsequently, she worked a day or two as a substitute teacher at the Somerton Grade School. Once when she was teaching my class she sent me and another boy outside to clean the blackboard erasers — we were probably talking and this was her way of getting rid of us. While cleaning the erasers we talked and laughed even more, which drew the attention of the first- and second-grade teacher, an old maid named Ada Gibbons who came out and said, "I'm sure if your father were alive, you'd be better behaved." It was a cruel and insensitive thing to say; I didn't like her much when she was my teacher and I liked her even less after that.

After only one year as the schoolmarm, Mom got a job in a

clothing factory in Barnesville and was able to get a ride to and from work with some other ladies working there. For a couple years she sewed the fly on boxer shorts that were supplied to sailors but later the factory changed its output to civilian work and made pajamas. Several times she managed to put the sewing machine needle through her finger and would come home with her finger painted brown with iodine. Mother was still working there when I finished college.

Transportation

TRANSPORTATION WAS ALWAYS A PROBLEM. Since we no longer had a car, we depended on neighbors. The bus ran twice daily between Barnesville and Woodsfield and cost 25 cents for a ride. The bus driver always told my family not to worry about putting a quarter into the fare box. The bus times were not always convenient, but we were never shy about asking someone if we could ride along if they were going to Barnesville. I would frequently ride along with someone just for the fun of going somewhere, anywhere. One of my favorite excursions was to Wheeling, West Virginia, where Fat Robert Gibbons went on a fairly regular basis to sell the chickens and eggs he had collected from farmers out in the country. A pickup full of chicken crates makes for a noisy and smelly ride. Going down into the Ohio Valley where coal smoke and smog made seeing even across the road difficult thwarted any possibility of keeping my shirt clean. There was also a strong sulfurous smell emanating from the smoking gob piles. One of Fat Robert's regular customers was a man with long hair, a black hat and a long black coat — a Jewish rabbi who slaughtered the chickens in a kosher manner. This involved holding the hapless bird by the neck over a pail of water and neatly slitting its throat with a gleaming straight razor. He probably said some ritualistic phrase as he was doing it, thus sanctifying the bird as kosher. The eye-opening thing to me was that there were actually living, breathing Jews. Up until then they existed only in the Bible as far as I knew.

Food

I DON'T THINK I EVER ATE STEAK until I was out of high school. We did have meat occasionally, especially on Sunday when a chicken would appear. We had other meat as well — hamburger or tuna fish, or a bologna sandwich. More often our sandwiches were simply mayonnaise or mustard spread onto a slice of Wonder Bread. Sometimes we had a slice of ham. Daddy looked forward to that so he could make "sop gravy" that consisted of deglazing the frying pan with some milk and boiling it down a bit. Vegetables were plentiful, too plentiful, mostly string beans and potatoes from our garden. Mother canned the beans, and we stored the potatoes in a small cellar under the house. We ate so many green beans that I avoid them to this day. I loved going to my grandmother's house because she always had Ritz crackers. Food became even more of a problem during World War II as sugar, flour, butter and many other things were rationed. The car windshield had a little sticker with a letter on it that indicated how much gasoline could be bought. We should have been thankful for the potatoes, but to raise a successful crop required a lot of weeding and hand picking the potato bugs off the plant's leaves. There were two types of potato bugs, a beetle type and a slug-like brown character. Naturally, taking care of the bugs was the job of us kids and consisted of crawling down the row of potato plants, pulling the insect off the leaves and dropping them into a coffee can of hot water that, of course, extinguished the critter.

We had a small quince tree and a sour cherry tree that provided pretty good jam. We also had a plum tree and brother Duane recalls having a very good crop of plums one year, which Mom canned. That particular year, after I had left home after high school, Duane shot a lot of squirrels, which provided many evening meals of fried squirrel and plums for him and Mom. Our nutrition was bolstered by the school lunch program, for which we were never appropriately thankful. We never had soda pop but occasionally Mom would let us make our own homemade version — vinegar, sugar, bicarbonate of soda and water, which made a nice fizzy drink. We would very rarely get a <u>pint</u> of ice cream from Bewley's and divide it among the five of us. I am still not particularly fond of strawberries after working a few weeks picking strawberries for a local farmer one summer. This job required me to crawl along the rows on wet grass and straw mulch so that it was difficult to stand up at the end of the day. Jim Mahoney and I were hired by another farmer to chop out the weeds in his cornfield with a hoe. This job paid 10 cents per row, and when he put us to work on a small plot we earned nearly two dollars for the day. When we went back the next day, he took us out to a much larger field where the rows seemed a half-mile long. After a long day of toil we had earned about 50 cents. I think we went back for one more day, but after that we said "forget it," even though he did give us lunch and keep us supplied with water.

The Garage and the Basketball Court

THE GARAGE THAT MY FATHER RAN between stints at the M & K grocery was next door to our house. It had been built shortly after the turn of the century using local materials including sand from Captina Creek for the cement blocks that constituted the walls. It was never much of a structure, although it was sturdy enough to have a cement floor in front and a wooden extension to the back where the cars could be driven for servicing. There was no indoor plumbing in our house or the garage. The lack of a toilet in the garage for the men and boys who frequented the place meant they simply used a designated corner of the building where the characteristic odor of stale urine was quite prominent. This is another of those things about scents and odors that left a lasting impression. Underneath the extended wooden floor, an area had been excavated that allowed access to the underside of a car and enabled removal of oil pans and other parts of a car's innards to be worked on. One of my jobs was to scrape out the congealed dirty oil from the oil pans or to scrub pistons with a wire brush dipped in gasoline. This got my hands as dirty as my nose after I carried in the coal to the school building. We had no use for the garage building after Daddy died and no one wanted to buy it so Mother arranged to have it torn down. My cousins and I did a lot of the work on the reachable parts of the walls and finally we were left with a concrete slab. This slab became a small basketball court when Fritz Stephens convinced my mother that a backboard with a basket and a net would be a good thing for the town's youth. The basketball court became a reality and was utilized heavily every day it didn't rain or snow. Jimmy Gibbons supplied the best basketball, but if that wasn't available we used a discarded one from the high school. This old grey ball seemed quite heavy and had all the bounce of a pumpkin. Everyone in town showed up to play and occasionally a fight broke out or things got so loud that Mom had to go out and shoo the boys away. We didn't have much team activity, but we did a lot of one-on- one and many a game of H-O-R-S-E taught us all to execute some fancy shots.

Hog Butchering

OUR HOUSE WAS A RICKETY OLD FRAME STRUCTURE with a sloping back porch. The house, like all the houses in Somerton, was situated along the one and only main street of the town — north-south oriented Ohio Route 8. Between the sidewalk, which in spite of the minuteness of the town was never rolled up at night, and the edge of the road was a 6-8-foot strip of grass. Behind the house were a couple of outbuildings and the privy, but not much of what one would call a lawn. The property sloped down to the back alley, which paralleled the main street. Beyond that the land sloped a quarter mile or so to the small crick, whereupon the land rose again until it gained the top of the ridge another quarter of a mile to the east. A similar configuration existed on the other side of the road. Our portion of this slope was given over to a garden, largely planted with potatoes and green beans that were stored in the root cellar or canned. The area beyond the alley was ostensibly a pasture, but also contained a few small barns and pig-pens and chicken coops. There was one large cavernous, several-story tobacco packinghouse on each back alley on both sides of the town. In addition to coal mining, the economic engine of that part of Appalachia was tobacco farming. Unfortunately, the fields of Kentucky and Virginia grew much better tobacco, and the tobacco packing and drying houses had been long abandoned except for use as storage. The ragweed and milkweed plants of the pasture crowded out the decent grass, so the fields were not prime grazing land by any means and would only support one, or at best, two scrawny cows.

It was in the pigpen belonging to a neighbor where the excitement seemed to originate on that cool, dark November morning. The Broomhall family had been up well before daylight to start a large fire that crackled and snapped and, when disturbed, sent sparks flying up into the mostly starless sky. By the time I wandered down to see what was happening in the corner of their lot next to ours, a large cauldron made from an oil drum and filled with water was bubbling over the fire and a heavy cloud of steam combined with the smoke from the wood fire made clear vision difficult. The smell of a crackling wood fire on an October or November night was familiar. The fire had been placed so as to be convenient to the stately walnut tree, one of whose lower branches would soon be utilized to anchor a block and tackle.

The Broomhall family consisted of Elder Broomhall, his son Earl who drove our school bus and whom we always referred to as Two-Gun Broomhall, and Earl's grown sons, Junior and Pickle. There was also a younger sister, Geraldine, but if any of the men had ever had a wife, no one had any recollection of it. Elder Broomhall was superintendent of the Sunday School at the Methodist church and no one had ever heard him swear, although he was frequently heard to say, "Oh, sugar, Junior," if he was particularly vexed at Junior. Junior had lost an eye somewhere in the course of his growing up and, in order to see, tilted his head, giving him an odd appearance of bewilderment and questions about who he was looking at. Pickle, who I'm sure had a different name on his birth certificate, was a rather ordinary character, but neither of the younger Broomhalls had a regular job that I was ever aware of and apparently subsisted on odd jobs. The family did collect rainwater for drinking and washing in a large barrel under the eaves of their shed, which attracted a lot of mosquitos. They grew a large garden and raised and processed their own meat and that's why we're here on this nippy November morning.

Two-Gun, Junior and Pickle entered the pigpen and sloshed around in the mud and pig shit to corner the largest of the three pigs. The pig realized that this was not going to go well, and resisted these efforts with grunts, squeals and attempts to bite and kick the Broomhalls. Ultimately the pig was brought down and his legs were quickly tied with short ropes, whereupon his throat was slit with a sharp knife that Junior pulled out of his back pocket. The squeals of the pig were horrendous and with each spasmodic jerk of his hog-tied body the bright red blood squirted out of his neck. Someone had produced an enameled wash pan and as much of the blood that wasn't spilled on the ground was collected in the pan for use in making blood sausage. Once the pig's death throes had ended, the carcass was dragged over to the walnut tree, hung up with the block and tackle and an additional wash pan used to collect more dripping blood, by now darkened. Then the carcass was swung over into the boiling cauldron to soften the hog bristles so they could be scraped off.

With the pig hanging over a large washtub, Two-Gun took a large, very sharp knife and made a long vertical slash on the pig's soft, white belly. Ropes of glistening yellow, white and red guts came tumbling out. These intestines would later be cleaned, washed out and used as sausage casings. The blackening red liver was set aside for further use. Butchering then began on the rest of the pig's carcass, with the legs being dismembered and put away for a few months, marinated and salt-rubbed to produce a salty savory ham. The lower flanks of the animal were cut in rectangular slabs and cured in a similar fashion to become bacon. The upper flanks were cut into similar slabs to be partly cooked and ultimately end up on the plate as spareribs. By now it was probably noon and a larger crowd had gathered, not to help, but to simply kibitz. The Broomhalls were not done. They proceeded to cut off the pig's head, declaring that they were going to make head cheese out of that. How this process develops, I have no idea. By this time there wasn't much left except the ears, hooves and the tail and, although modern slaughterhouses use these parts as well, they were discarded. We did salvage the pig's bladder, which when blown up with air makes a fairly decent soccer ball, and the less useful of us went down the alley kicking our new soccer ball. We were far from alone in putting this part of the pig to good use.

In the 1970's, Edna Lewis wrote a cookbook based on her experiences as a black woman cook, called *The Edna Lewis Cookbook*. One passage that engaged me was a passage titled "Hog Killing." Lewis recalled the day each fall when her family would turn pigs into pork — "It's not gruesome, but it is earthy." It is still grounding to read these lines, "My Father would remove the liver and the bladder, which he would present to us. We would blow up the bladders with straws cut from reeds and hang them in the house to dry. By Christmas they would have turned transparent like beautiful balloons. The following morning my brothers and sisters and I would rush out before breakfast to see the hogs hanging from the scaffolds like giant statues. The hogs looked beautiful. They were glistening white inside with their lining of fat, and their skin was almost translucent."

Killing what we ate was a part of growing up in that era and place. Anyone who has ever plucked a chicken will recognize the stench of wet, matted chicken feathers after such an immersion, but the pig scalding with the accompanying steam and blood is much more memorable. For those of you who get their chickens neatly packed in a plastic bag, sans feathers and the gizzard, kidneys and liver tidily stuffed into the chicken's carcass, chicken plucking is probably something you have been spared in your development. It's also noteworthy that chicken was only eaten on Sunday in Appalachia, and I was occasionally dispatched on a Sunday morning after services at the Methodist church to the neighbors with a 25-cent piece to pay for the chicken Mr. Detling selected from his small flock. I then proceeded to bring the unlucky fowl to our backyard, where I dispatched her with a hatchet and dunked the carcass in a bucket of boiling water preparatory to plucking the feathers off. There really is such a thing as a chicken with its head cut off who tries to run and hops around a few seconds after it's decapitated.

The Farmers' Institute

SOMERTON WAS A STRICTLY RURAL COMMUNITY. Not much in the way of community activities happened save for the Election Day chicken dinners put on by the ladies of the Methodist church featuring chicken fricassee and homemade pies. Occasionally a parade for the Fourth of July was organized, but was by no means an annual event. What was an annual event was the agricultural fair more commonly known as the Farmers' Institute. This day-long extravaganza was held in the high school gymnasium/auditorium and usually featured an appearance by the county agricultural agent and, in an election year, an aspiring county sheriff or a congressman (the most notorious was Wayne L. Hayes, who was subsequently run out of the House of Representatives after a dalliance with an apparently well-known Washington, D.C., stripper). The Farmers' Institute was essentially a small-scale country fair, although there were no rides or carnival barkers, simply ladies displaying their quilts, jellies and jams and the farmers showing off their huge pumpkins or large ears of corn. There were other exhibits of varying kinds. Perhaps one of the more unusual ones was the entry of a stuffed raccoon by my brother Duane.

He had taken a correspondence course in taxidermy and when he happened upon a raccoon, he stuffed it and entered it in the Farmers' Institute. He took first prize for "most unusual entry." Somewhere along the way, my father had acquired a stuffed red squirrel that provided the décor for our small living room along with a few family photos and a picture of Jesus on the wall. I usually got some benefit from the institute because they sponsored a contest amongst the schoolchildren to make posters advertising the event. I was a bit ahead of the crowd artistically, so usually won the poster prize. Brother David decided one year that he would join the 4-H club and announced that his project would be a field of corn. This was a bit audacious as we didn't have any land to grow corn, but when the 4-H leaders came around to see how the project was coming he simply took them over to inspect the neighbor's cornfield.

Tooting Our Horns

TEMPERANCEVILLE, as has been mentioned, was even smaller than Somerton, but they did have a St. Mary's picnic in the summer that galvanized he whole town. It was a hot summer day and the Somerton High School Band had been engaged to provide some musical entertainment. We were gathered together, ready to play, when our bass drummer, a resident of Temperanceville, arrived and was obviously already in the spirit of the occasion, whereupon Mr. Gates the band director sent him home as too drunk to play. We were probably into our second number when Paul Poulton, the drummer, staggered up to the front of the ensemble and decked Mr. Gates! After dusting himself off, Mr. Gates led us through a couple more numbers, and we got back on the school bus and retreated to more civil climes.

Our band had a rather interesting evolution. When I was in the sixth grade, someone decided our school should have a band. It turned out that a town down the road, Powhatan Point, had used band uniforms of more or less the right purple and gold color and a band director available to us as a part-time director. When it was firmly decided that we should have a band, a man from a nearby town, Quaker City, who sold and rented band instruments showed up with an array of instruments and laid them out in the parking lot of the grade school, a display not unlike the displays of pies and quilts at the Farmers' Institute. The sight of the trombone in its purple-lined case was too much for me to resist. I wanted that trombone, but the $45 price was more than Mom could afford. Further, Margaret Jean wanted a trumpet and David felt he was destined to play the clarinet. I don't know how much moaning and groaning I did, but after a few days, my mother found the $45 and I was started on a career as a trombone player. That skill has stuck with me most of my life and I still occasionally play, but not very well. This wasn't the only time she magically found a few dollars to support a project that was important to us, and to her.

Silk Hat Harry and the Bank

SOMERTON WASN'T ALWAYS SO SMALL AND POOR. At one time it had a bank, a Grange Hall and a Masonic Hall. In addition to the Masons there was a club called the Knights of Pythias to which my father belonged. I don't know exactly what they did, but I suspect that there was some liquor involved. The Grange Hall was built shortly after the Civil War and was the headquarters for a farmers' organization called the Grange. That organization gradually dwindled away and the hall was given over to such civic enterprises as a polling place on Election Day, town meeting facility or an occasional movie. During World War II, the hall was used as a collection point for all the zinc jar lids, milkweed pods and foil gum wrappers we had collected to aid the war effort and a place where the women of the town sewed and rolled bandages and even made cotton tick mattresses. On Election Day in November, a chicken dinner was served from the Masonic Hall across the street. It was the bank that attracted the attention of a man who showed up in town in 1902 and expressed interest in settling down in Somerton and establishing a business. He was obviously a bit out of character with his fancy clothes and a tall hat that gave him the name of Silk Hat Harry. He attracted a good deal of curiosity among the townspeople, who were excited about some of the prospects he was mentioning.

A night or two after the arrival of Silk Hat Harry, Earle Wilson, the postmaster who lived across the street from the bank, was awakened by a muffled explosion that seemed to come from the vicinity of the bank itself. Mr. Wilson ran outside in time to see two men get into a carriage parked in front of the bank and take off at a high rate of speed. As you have probably guessed, Silk Hat Harry and a confederate had blown the bank's safe and made off with its contents. A posse was quickly formed and chased the carriage south along Route 8, enlisting the help of the Monroe County sheriff as they passed through Woodsfield and actually got close enough to the robbers to fire a few ineffectual shots. The chase ended at the Ohio River, where the desperados leapt into a waiting boat and rowed to freedom on the West Virginia side.

The Bull and the Dog

NOT TOO MANY MEMORIES REMAIN from our residence in the house where I was born, but one of my earliest memories was when we still lived in the house and the house across the street burned down even for a rather young child. A frame house burning at night makes an unforgettable sight. Since there was no fire department in our village about all that could be done was for everyone to stand around and watch her burn. They probably tried a bucket brigade but without a significant source of water that wouldn't succeed. Not long after that when I was perhaps 5 and my sister Margaret Jean was 4, we slipped out of the house and went into the woods behind the house. Who knows where we thought we were going, but we were supposed to be taking an afternoon nap, resting up for a Fourth of July parade later in the day. We were accompanied by our beagle Hotshot, a dog I loved. It wasn't long before my parents realized that we had escaped and an APB went through the town. By this time, we had ventured far enough into the woods and the adjacent field to have encountered a bull, an enormous creature with a ring in his nose and brass balls on the ends of his horns. The bull pawed the earth threatening two little kids — scared out of their wits by this time — but the bull was being kept at bay by the beagle. Fortunately, one of the young men of the town found us before the bull realized that the beagle was really no match for him. Needless to say, we were punished by being confined to our room and probably put to bed without supper as well as forgoing the Fourth of July parade.

Mother and Father

MY MOTHER, ANNA FORNI LUCAS, was a rather serious person who didn't tolerate some of my more free-spirited father's antics. I remember rather vividly going up to Barnesville with him on some errand or another, but Daddy, after his business was completed, stopped at the local pool hall and got into a backroom poker game while I lay on a cold leather couch in the pool hall. Mother wasn't pleased when we got home well after midnight — whether my father won or lost is of no consequence — and told him that if he ever kept me out that late again the marriage was at an end. Most of the time though, things seemed to go along fairly well with occasional trips to Canton or Bethesda to visit relatives, and what I particularly liked were the trips to local creeks or lakes for fishing trips. I do remember though, that my mother was frequently admonishing my father to slow down as he drove the curving roads of southeastern Ohio in his Willys Knight or an early model Plymouth. How fast one of those cars could go I can't really say.

We would occasionally go fishing where Daddy would drive the car up to a flat spot near a large crick or the Muskingum River, and he would seriously fish while we kids would frolic in the water. This is how we learned to swim — no swim lessons or neighborhood pool swim teams for us. Sometime when were quite small, several men of the town got together and bought a piece of riverfront property on the Muskingum River about 40 miles from Somerton. The Muskingum is not much of a river, but it did ultimately empty into the Ohio. A cooperative effort of the men of Somerton, including Charles "Hud" Maghee, resulted in a fairly large fishing camp where we would go for a week or so in the summer with some of the other families. Hud Maghee, his brother Hoss and their mother, "Aunt H," were the only African-Americans in the town. Actually, they lived in a simple frame house up on one of the ridges so, except for Hoss, were rarely seen.

When I went to Barnesville for my final year of high school, there were two black kids in my class of 98: Bob Lucas, a bruising fullback on our football team, and Shirley Bell, who later became a nurse. When I went back to Barnesville High as the graduation speaker some 50 years later, I asked the school superintendent how many kids were getting their diplomas — still 98! Not much growth but fortunately not many losses either.

The fishing camp was one large room with a high ceiling, wooden floors and, of course, no indoor toilet or running water. There was a kitchen in one corner and beds for the adults in one end of the building and more beds for the children at the other end of the room. These beds were metal frame jobs with a straw mattress. Try sleeping on that sometime. In the quiet of the night, the silence, except for the hoot owls and stray dogs, was frequently interrupted by the scurrying of mice around the cabin. A lot of the fishing was done by stringing trotlines across the river, no challenge to the fisherman's skills once the line and hooks were set. I apparently was apprehended in the middle of the night one time when I went sleepwalking to check the trotlines. The trotline method allowed plenty of time during the day for Daddy to sit on the small front porch and spit tobacco juice over the rail. The grown-ups would check the line twice a day and often lugged a huge catfish out of the water or the occasional eel or turtle that had grabbed onto the baited hook. We kids loved being out there in the "wilderness," and the grown-ups seemed to have a great time drinking beer and playing poker.

The Heights and School Beginnings

WHILE WE WERE LIVING IN THE SMALL HOME where I was born, my father was busy converting a defunct creamery into a house about a quarter of a mile up the hill. This turned out to be a rather classy place by our standards — it even had indoor plumbing. We lived there for a couple years, and that is where we were living when I was hit by the bicycle. This house was on the steepest part of the road that constituted the main street of Somerton, so that the kid who hit me with the bike had a good head of steam up as he coasted down the hill. I wonder if he got hurt? I don't recall that he did, but I certainly remember the multicolored adhesive plasters Doc Johnson put on my various abrasions. About the time I was old enough to start first grade — there was no kinder-garten in our area at that time — we moved eight miles up the road to the larger town of Barnesville, where my Dad had taken a job as a mechanic at the M & K Grocery Company. School didn't start there till a week or so later than Somerton, and I was very disappointed not to be starting school with my friends. The trauma was compounded when I showed up at the new school in Barnesville, knowing no one, and entered the classroom that was one desk short. I didn't have a place to sit but, of course, this was soon taken care of, and I began my educational experience. I soon made some friends as well as a couple of enemies, and pro-gressed through the school year under the tutelage of Mrs. Oliver. My aunt, Lottie Forni, the quintessential old maid, taught third grade in the school and that didn't make things any easier because she felt responsible for monitoring my behavior. That tendency stayed with her regarding me and my brothers and sister till we were at least 35 years of age.

We had rented a large house on Broadway, for us a veritable mansion. It had an adequate number of bedrooms and indoor plumbing! For some reason I can still remember the green marble fireplace in the living room. At the end of the school year Daddy decided we should move back to Somerton, where he had bought the garage and the house next door. This house where I spent the next 11 years till I finished high school was really pretty sad. Its only good feature was the front porch, which was big enough for not only a glider but also a porch swing. The house had a living room, a kitchen with water available if you were willing to grab the pump handle, and a small dining room on the first floor. The kitchen led to a small porch that

> HONOR ROLL
> SOMERTON SCHOOL
> Grades 1 and 2
> Adda Gibbons, teacher
> Grade 1 — Nancy Burcher 96 3/12, Brenda Morrison 95 4/12, Ruth Tulga 93 8/12, Betty Davis 93 4/12, Robert Steele 92 9/12.
> Grade 2 — Linda Skinner 94 4/12, Donna Pickens 93 9/12, Jack Howell 93 7/12, Donald Froehlich 91 4/12, Linda Wharton 91 3/12.
>
> Grade 3 and 4
> Lela Mahoney, teacher
> Grade 3—Virginia Mae Froehlich 99, Myrna Kaye Timmons 97¾, Phyllis Jefferis 95¼, Gene Burga 91, Gerald Tulga 90½.
> Grade 4—Neal Mahoney 94 4/5, Joann Howell 94 3/5, Robert Hagan 91 4/5.
>
> Grade 5 and 6
> Olive Detling, teacher
> Grade 5—Margaret Jean Lucas 98½, Mary Ellen Jefferis 97 2/3, Danny Lee Hagan 95 2/3, Roger Ackerman 95 1/3, James Robert Gibbons 95, William Hyett 90 2/3.
> Grade 6—Janet Huntsman 93½, George Lucas 97 2/3, Jewell Huntsman 96, James Mahoney 92, Norman Carter 90 1/6.
>
> Grade 7 and 8
> Marie Grimes, teacher
> Grade 7—William Quinn 95 4/5, Shirley Mann 94 3/5, Nell Hagan 91.
> Grade 8—Geraldine Broomhall 90.

Margaret Jean and George Lucas made the news in fifth and sixth grades.

tilted 20 degrees to the south and was very rickety. There were two bedrooms upstairs and a landing area at the top of the stairs that served as another bedroom. The bed in that ersatz bedroom was right up against windows that weren't very well insulated. More than once I awoke on a winter morning with snow on the covers. The house was heated by a fireplace in the living room and a gas heater, also in the living room. We all gathered in front of the living room heater to get dressed for school on winter mornings, the firepit having been covered with coal the evening before to keep it smoldering through the night. We didn't have any window shades or heavy curtains, but if some passerby looked into the house and saw three or four kids in their underwear, so be it. The gas that came from a well outside of town wasn't of very high quality and it tended to leak from around the fittings on the heater, so it's amazing that gas or perhaps carbon monoxide from the smoldering fireplace didn't kill us all. Occasionally, the gas pressure was so low that we couldn't get enough heat out of the gas range to boil water and Mom would phone Tom Lambert who operated the well and ask him to go loosen up a valve or whatever he did to improve the gas service. Shortly after we moved into the Somerton house, Daddy hired Hud Maghee, who was a handyman and bricklayer, to build a fireplace. It was a fine fireplace made of white bricks that, unfortunately, Daddy had a tendency to stain when the spit from his chaw of Red Man chewing tobacco didn't quite make it onto the fire. As part of the fireplace construction, they made a large, vertical cabinet on the side that came to hold my father's shotgun, my untrustworthy rifle, an old Spanish-American War musket and a couple fishing poles, although most of our fishing was done with a cane pole. Hud was a very hardworking man who could fix or build anything, while Hoss worked for a local farmer and, as far as I know, never took a sober breath. Still, he was a good worker. When Hoss came to town on Sunday morning, all the town dogs congregated to bark and escort him to the bench in front of Bewley's store, where he sat, ready to talk to anyone who came along. Attempts to reform him from his drinking habit were never successful. It was said that he could ride through Barnesville on the back of a hay wagon and by the time the journey through town was complete someone, somehow had slipped him a pint of whiskey.

Have I mentioned a bathroom in the Somerton house? Step out into the back yard where the privy stood. We were not very affluent and thus had only a one-holer where we used newspaper to wipe our butts. Some people tried to use pages from the Spiegel or Sears, Roebuck catalogue, but that paper is too stiff and slick, although that particular paper was plentiful as every household received a large copy of the catalogue each and every year. One could order virtually anything from the catalogue — shoes, dresses, fishing rods, baseball gloves and even the material to build a pre-fab house. We didn't have to go out there at night though, as we utilized a chamber pot in the largest bedroom and for the boys, a "pee can" such as a large juice can or coffee can. Privacy? Forget it!

My father shaved at the kitchen sink with a straight razor, which always looked quite lethal to me. He would occasionally nick himself and require a touch-up with a styptic pencil to stop the bleeding. Water for washing and shaving and tooth brushing was produced by a few cranks on the pump handle and heated in a teakettle.

The razor itself was sharpened by a few swipes across the leather razor strop, which occasionally had other purposes. The back porch did occasionally serve as a launching pad for a pee, saving a trip to the outhouse. Baths were a Saturday night occasion when a washtub was placed in the middle of the kitchen or, in winter, in front of the fireplace and water from the teakettle was used to provide a little warmth to the bath. Once we got to high school, we would take showers there after basketball practice or after gym class — definitely a luxury.

Single-Parent Families

THERE'S NO QUESTION that having two loving parents is optimum for child raising, but it is possible to grow up without a criminal bent with only one parent, in my case my mother. As a matter of fact, brother Duane never knew his father at all, having been born a month after Daddy had died. We received a great deal of support, particularly from my Grandmother Forni, as well as from aunts and uncles and older cousins. For example, my cousin Francis Brock when he came back from three years on a U.S. Navy sub chaser in the South Pacific during WWII coming over and painting our house.

Francis and the Brocks

I GREW UP A TIME LONG BEFORE anyone ever thought of Disneyland or Worlds of Fun. We never went on what one would call a vacation, but frequently piled into our old car and went a few miles to Barnesville to my grandmother's house, to Bethesda to visit relatives on the other side of the family or to Speidel to visit our cousins the Brocks. We occasionally made a longer trip (80 miles) to visit my other grandmother and additional cousins, aunts and uncles in Canton, Ohio. Often after such visits in the summer, one of us would be left behind to spend a couple weeks on the Brock farm or in the city with my Grandmother Okey. It was during one of those times when I was at the Brock farm with my cousins Madeline and Robert that their older brother Francis came back home after his service in the U.S. Navy. Francis had enlisted at age 18 shortly after the war broke out and spent several years as a bosun's mate on a submarine chaser tooling around the Pacific and occasionally engaging a Japanese submarine or some other small vessel. We all wanted to hear about his adventures in the war, but he was reluctant to talk much about that. He would occasionally demonstrate various commands for us by blowing on his bosun's pipe but that was about as close as we got to his Navy service. He seemed determined to make up for lost time with the ladies of the area. Nearly every evening he would clean up and dose himself with cologne, get in the Brocks' old Chevy and disappear till 3 or 4 o'clock in the morning. We didn't have a chance to talk to him the next morning as he usually slept till noon. There wasn't a whole lot for him to do around the small farm, so my mother hired him to paint our house. She agreed to pay him an amount equal to what he spent on paint, so he took the job and finished in a week. I don't think that he was particularly scathed by the war, but it did seem to take him awhile to get his life together. He ultimately took advantage of the GI Bill and got a college degree and worked for an electric company for most of his life. In later years he repaired television sets and fished, thus becoming a master fisherman. His brother Lewis, two years older, was a civilian employee of the U.S. Air Force and absorbed, I'm sure, a lot of radiation photographing the atom bomb tests at Bikini Atoll and Enewetak.

My mother's older sister, Alberta, and her husband, Harry, had a small subsistence farm down in a holler near Speidel, Ohio. The Brock farm was remote enough that on the rare occasion that a car went down the road that divided the farm into an upper and lower segment, all hands turned out to get a glimpse of the car and speculate on its destination and the occupants. They had enough hilly land to support 10 or so cows, which provided a meager income. Otherwise they lived off the land, with sweet corn, potatoes, green beans, milk, of course, and eggs gathered from a few freely roaming chickens. Occasionally one of the chickens found itself in a pot on the stove, as did a rabbit or squirrel that had been blasted with the family shotgun. Every year or so, the cowherd produced a male calf that would be raised for beef. One year the calf was a particularly appealing one, and Uncle Harry said he didn't think he could bring himself to butcher it when the time came. My macho father said, "No problem. We'll take him and raise him, and I won't have any trouble killing and butchering him." The calf, by now named Tiny, came back to our house. The neighbor at an adjacent farm allowed us to keep Tiny in his fenced-in field, where we kids took very good care of him with plenty of food and water. Finally, the day of his demise arrived, and despite my father's early bravado, Tiny was taken away for someone else to kill and butcher. We never did have a lot of food in our house, but Mother couldn't tempt us with any of the hamburger or beef stew that came from Tiny.

The best part of the Brock farm was in the flat bottomland between two fairly steep hillsides. There was just enough tillable land to support a small cornfield and a hay field. When the hay was ready in mid-summer, Uncle Harry mowed it and raked it with his horse and mower. Tractors were for the bigger farms. A crick meandered through the bottom and was wide enough in a couple places for us to go swimming if we didn't mind sharing with the water snakes. Basically, we were skinny-dipping but we could never persuade Madeline to fully participate. One day that is etched in my memory, we were getting out of the water when we were confronted by a large skunk standing on the bank. The smell of a skunk was familiar, but the sight of that creature with flies buzzing all around him made us wonder if we were ever going to get out of the swimming hole. We were very careful not to agitate him, and he finally ambled off into the brush. Not only did he smell, but he was filthy and nowhere as attractive as the pristine black-and-white-striped characters of the comics.

If you are going to have a dairy farm, you'll need a barn, which the Brocks had and which was more commodious than their small house. It was nice and warm in the mornings and evenings when cows were being milked and the cats were milling around hoping for a squirt of milk. There was a large hayloft where we could hide and jump off the upper floors to the piles of hay below. Surprisingly, there were no injuries to any of us. In addition to relying on the land for food, fuel for the kitchen stove and heating the house was sourced locally. A shallow vein of bituminous coal poked out of the hillside and occasionally Uncle Harry would go up there with a wheelbarrow, a pick and a shovel and dig up the coal that he needed. Farm families get up early in the morning but also go to bed early, essentially when it got dark. It's hard to read or sew much by the light of a kerosene lamp.

In spite of its out of the way location, the Brock farm was a place where all the family frequently gathered for holidays or to welcome my mother's brothers Robert and Charles when they came to visit. Neither of them had finished high school and found their way to Silver Spring, Maryland, a D.C. suburb, where they worked, got married and, in the case of Charles, raised one daughter. They made the 300-mile trip back to Ohio occasionally, bringing home movies, oysters to use in oyster stew and a block of ice to use in the hand-cranked ice cream maker. We kids loved to take turns cranking the machine and looked forward to when the ice cream was done and we could lick the dasher. Cranking the machine required someone to sit on top of the ice cream maker, insulated somewhat by a folded burlap bag placed over the ice in the bucket, but it still didn't take long before your butt was cold and wet. If you wanted to have a turn at the crank, it was obligatory to take a shift as "an ice sitter."

Aunt Anne, Poker and Animals

MY AUNT ANNE, my father's half sister, taught me a lot of things and I was always amazed at what she knew, having never finished high school, and what she could do. She was a true Auntie Mame and when my mother couldn't quite cope with me when I was 14 and 15 years old, Aunt Anne took me to her house in Canton for two summers. She and her third husband, Uncle Penny, a fireman and former Marine Corps major, owned and operated a pet shop and we lived, literally, with the animals. The three-story house had a large kitchen on the first floor and bedrooms and baths on the second and third floors, but the rest of the building was given over to bird cages, fish tanks and pens for cats, puppies, monkeys, guinea pigs and other small creatures. The dogs, and they were several, ranging from a huge Great Dane to small Boston Terriers, had the run of the place. Although there was a backyard where they often roamed around and dug holes in the dirt, they frequently managed to shit inside. Aunt Anne not only sold puppies, snakes, fish, birds, monkeys and so on, but also raised and showed the aforementioned dogs. Not just any old dogs either but those with a pedigree that got them into places like the Westminster Kennel Club shows. Thus the house was full of these Great Danes, Boston Terriers and regular bulldogs who shat a lot, and I mean a lot. Naturally, one of my jobs was to clean up the dog shit. That can sour one on being a dog lover pretty quick. Thank goodness there were no pit bulls! Birds can be quite messy too and, of course, parrots and macaws can inflict some rather painful bites. Fish tend to be a lot easier to deal with.

Aunt Anne smoked a pack and a half of cigarettes a day,

drank several Seagram's 7 high balls as well during the workday and swore like a truck driver. She could hold her own in any business deal and especially at the poker table. She was very confident and successful with her suppliers and customers. I learned a lot about preparedness and confidence from observing her operate. We did quite a lot of local traveling to buy fish, birds, animals and supplies and would go to Akron, Columbus, Cleveland or Pittsburgh with some regularity. A couple of times while in Cleveland or Pittsburgh, she would take the afternoon off and we would go to an Indians or Pirates baseball game, a great treat for a kid from Somerton. She also owned a drive-in restaurant, and we would frequently go there for supper, as she was not about to cook. This was much more exciting stuff than the regular fare at home in Somerton or what Aunt Anne's cook and housekeeper, Nixeola, would come up with. Even though it was typical drive-in fare — hamburgers, hot dogs, fries etc. — it was definitely a treat for me. One painful experience from that time was when I came down with strep throat and had to have a series of penicillin shots. I lay in my bed upstairs and the doctor would come every day and inject a wad of penicillin into my tender butt. A similar confinement occurred when I was 11 or so and developed an ear infection that Doc Johnson couldn't cure. I was shipped off to my Aunt Dena's house in Bridgeport, across the river from Wheeling so we could go to the Wheeling Clinic. There, an ENT doctor probed my ear daily and eradicated the infection. Aunt Dena's friends were amazed when they came over to see me reading a book or the *Reader's Digest*, as apparently their children weren't very enthusiastic readers. This visit to Aunt Dena's gave me another of life's lessons similar to my discovery of the living Jew — racial prejudice! Aunt Dena gave me money to go to the movies at the air-conditioned theater down the street. I paid my money, went in and sat down in the back row of the theater. I had just gotten comfortable when the usher came by and said I had to move up front — only the "colored" people sat in the back. My brother David was far more of a challenge to my mother than I was, so Aunt Anne took him on for the last two years he was in high school, and not just for the summer. Aunt Anne was a bit of a character, and was married three times.

Genetic Material

AUNT ANNE WAS MY FATHER'S HALF-SISTER. It seems that my father was conceived out of wedlock, as they used to say, and so his name was Lucas, as opposed to the children who came later when my Grandmother Alda Lucas married Mr. Okey and had five Okey children named, respectively Ed, Frank, John, Warren and Anne. It has recently come to light that my great-grandfather, David Lucas, owned some land near Somerton that is now thought to harbor oil and gas reserves a drilling company is eager to tap into but first has to get rid of any claims to the land from myriad descendants, including me. Mr. Okey made a trip to the Klondike at the time of the gold rush. He actually struck it rich there and came back to the neighboring town of Bethesda as a very prosperous citizen. Unfortunately, when he died, my unsophisticated grandmother was gradually swindled out of the family holdings and had to go to work rolling cigars in a cigar factory. I call him Mr. Okey here although I never met him and didn't know his first name until recently (John W.). My other grandmother, Mollie Workman Forni, came from an English background, as did the Lucases, while Grandfather Forni was of French-German descent. There are records of Lucases going back at least to the time of Henry the Eighth in England. The Forni side was much more pious than the Okeys or the Lucases, and none of them would ever let a taste of beer cross their lips.

Grandmother Forni with, clockwise from left, Anna Forni Lucas, Dena Forni Cook, Lottie Forni and Alberta Forni Brock.

My grandfather, George Forni, for whom I was named, didn't speak English till he started school. My great-grandfather emigrated from Alsace-Lorraine in France, a particular piece of real estate that changed hands a few times over the centuries and in the early 1800's was a German-speaking region, so George Forni spoke German. There are still plenty of German influences in that part of France, but they now speak French and make excellent French wine. The name Forni may even be Italian, as we found out when we looked through the telephone books of the area one summer. I was spending the summer of 1983 as a visiting surgeon at the Kantonspital in Basel, Switzerland, and we took the two youngest children with us to live in a small apartment in Binningen, one of the Basel suburbs. Our oldest daughter, Diane, took a week off from her studies in Paris to visit us. Since she spoke fairly good

French by that time, we went to Alsace to search out the ancestors and thus ended up looking through all the phone books in Alsace-Lorraine for Fornis. We found only one family and when we phoned them they indicated that their family origin was Italy.

Grandma Forni was a very serious little woman who worked hard. She was especially kind to us children, as most grandmothers are, and we spent a lot of time at her house. She, Grandpa and Aunt Lottie lived in a very small house in Barnesville. They really didn't have an extra bedroom so we fought over who got the couch and who had to sleep on the floor in the living room. This was nice because it was close to the fireplace but a hard place to sleep as the clock on the mantel chimed every 15 minutes. Grandpa was deaf as a post, but he was a busy guy and probably the most frugal person I've ever met. He saved everything. Bent nails were straightened, papers were folded and stacked, turkey feathers from the Thanksgiving bird were saved as, were eggshells. Nails I can understand but why he saved eggshells I have no idea. All of these activities occurred in the little shop he had behind the house. Perhaps the most unusual collection was a large ball of string. He lived about half a mile from the railroad track where a passing freight train dropped a piece of string on the track twice a day, as a form of early communication between the station and the engineer of the train. When the train was due, the station-master stood by the side of the track and held up a forked stick that had a piece of paper attached to the string across the fork of the stick. The engineer grabbed the string, read the message and dropped the string onto the side of the track a few yards further on. My grandfather would go by regularly and pick up the string, thus collecting a fairly sizeable ball of string. Grandpa suffered from dyspepsia most of his life and when someone told him that goat's milk would help that, he promptly bought two goats and kept them tied up at the back corner of the lot. They were good milk producers, so when we visited he insisted we have a glass of goat's milk. Whether it eased my grandfather's stomach distress, I don't recall but after a couple of years the goats were gone.

Winter

THERE WAS A LOT OF SNOW AND ICE in southeastern Ohio in the winters of 1949, '50 and '51. The lake, really a pond, froze over and enough snow piled on Ohio Route 8 that we could bobsled down through Somerton at night. Someone produced a long, wooden bobsled that would accommodate perhaps 10 of us, and we would start at the top of Somerton hill, whiz through the flat part of town and continue down below town to the bridge over Captina Creek, some mile and a half to two miles down the road, where the bobsled glided to a stop. We could only make a couple of runs an evening given the difficulties of getting the heavy wooden sled back up to the top of the hill. One of the great things about growing up in a small town — not enough traffic on Route 8 to worry us about barreling down the middle of the highway, though I don't quite know what we might have done if a car or truck appeared. If we weren't bobsledding, we were skating on the pond. The ice was thick enough for us to build a bonfire right on the ice out of old tires and skate the night away. I don't recall anyone falling through the ice or breaking an ankle, and we had no other motive than to have fun.

One evening my friend Jimmie Gibbons went skating with us against the orders of his father, known to us as Fat Robert. When he realized that Jim was missing, he came down to the lake to get him. Jim, still with his skates on, was running up the hill pursued by Fat Robert yelling and huffing and puffing. Unfortunately, Jim had to cross a fence and with his skates on, couldn't quite navigate the obstacle and was caught by Fat Robert, who administered a thrashing then and there.

The state highway that divided our town into houses and small businesses on one side of the road from a similar grouping on the other side was used as a playground and particularly as a football field. Traffic wasn't much of a problem and if we heard a car or truck coming, we simply suspended play for a few seconds and allowed them to pass.

Memories Brewing

IT'S NOW FATHER'S DAY 2015. I did something today that almost always reminds me of my father. It's beastly hot today, as it frequently is in the summer in Kansas, so after working in the garden a bit, I eagerly popped the cap on a frosty bottle of beer. I don't drink a lot of beer but the smell of beer on a hot day usually is a Proustian moment. My father's half brothers all lived in Canton, Ohio, where they worked either for the post office or the Timken Roller Bearing company. In the fall they would all get together and come down to Belmont County to hunt squirrels. They would either establish a campsite on the banks of Captina Creek or rent rooms at Josie Lucas' (no relation) Dew Drop Inn. Josie was a large-breasted woman who had apparently inherited a large house when her husband left her. The house had been a mansion owned by the town's wealthiest citizen when the town was more prosperous. The original owner, as befitting his status, had extensive gardens and lawns around the property where, when Josie owned it, the town would be entertained with an ice cream social after the annual Memorial Day or Fourth of July parade. One of the treasures of the property was a large Ginko tree, apparently imported from Japan. Over the decades it grew to become, allegedly, the largest tree in the state of Ohio. She turned the large house into a hotel and would occasionally attract guests such as my uncles, although Somerton was certainly not a tourist destination. The uncles and the older cousins would always have plenty of beer and I would smell it when Daddy would go to join them and I would tag along. They wouldn't give me any beer to drink, but I certainly could inhale the fumes!

Pseudonyms

IT SEEMS LIKE EVERYONE I KNEW growing up had a nickname. Why that was such a common thing, I don't know, but there were Two-Gun, Junior and Pickle Broomhall. Josie Lucas was known as Duck Foot Sue. I was occasionally referred to as Leviticus, but mostly I was simply Luke or Georgie, which I hated because of the nursery rhyme that followed my being called Georgie or even Georgie Porgie ...

"Georgie Porgie, pudding and pie. Kissed the girls and made them cry; When the boys came out to play, Georgie Porgie ran away."

Margaret Jean was often called Pear Shape for no apparent good reason, and David was know as Pie Cutter with equally obscure origins. Duane was known as Butch. Margaret's friend, Alice Mae, was known as Slugger, probably for good reason, and she was living with her grandparents, Frog and Genelly Hunter. My good friend Jim Gibbons was known as Briggs, apparently in reference to the black man from Barnesville who was the local junk dealer, Mr. Briggs. Jim wasn't dark but his teeth were definitely black, apparently due to decay brought on by eating too much candy. His father, Fat Robert, owned the general store and candy was readily available to little Jimmie. His younger brother, Charles, was always Chud or Chuddie. Jim's Uncle Howard was known as Chibble. Robert Byers, the high school principal, was known to all of us as Tucky, but nobody ever called him that to his face. For some reason his sons Bobby, Billy and Donnie were immune to any additional appellations. I spent a lot of time with the Byers boys, and it was through their back lot that we were able to access the small pond or lake behind the town where we swam and fished in the summer and ice-skated in the winter. The Byers family lived in a large house formerly owned by a previous town doctor. I don't know the circumstances of the doctor leaving the house to the Byers, but he left all his medical books in the attic. We were forbidden to go into the attic, but there were ways to get there without Hazel Byers knowing about our whereabouts. We learned a bit about genital anatomy from looking in these books, although we should have been scared to see all the sores, ulcers and pustules that were illustrated. This was a time when medical books were beautifully illustrated by artists and before photographs were utilized.

Fred Stephens, the history teacher and coach (aren't all coaches history teachers?) was referred to as Fritz, which certainly makes some sense in view of his given name. His next-door neighbor, Willard Mann, was known to one and all as Sock Mann. I have mentioned Fatty Warton whose real name, Clyde, I never heard used. He operated one of the small grocery stores in town serving the upper end of the town while Gibbons' store and Bewley's store served the middle of the town a stone's throw apart from each other. Bewley's was the more prosperous one, having a gas tank out front that dispensed gasoline from a large glass cylinder. They also had the U.S. Post Office, which ensured that everyone would drop in at least once a day. The mail was brought from Barnesville in a little green truck. My grandfather frequently hitched a ride and came to Somerton to help out with various chores around our house. He seemed to think that part of his responsibilities was to monitor the behavior of us grandchildren, which we really didn't appreciate. Bewley's store was a half block north of our house and at a slightly higher elevation, so that for a time when the gas pump sprung a leak, the water in our house had a distinct taste and smell of Esso. Apparently a little contamination of that sort is not all that harmful. Bewley's store was founded by Buck Bewley, whose son Mumbles and his grandson Meathands ran the store. Another son, Donnie, didn't enter the store business and after a short stint in the Marine Corps went to Ohio University, got a degree and returned to Somerton as a history teacher. Fortunately for him, the coaching duties were all taken up by Fritz Stephens and he could concentrate on his teaching. Apparently he was never assigned an alias. The store must have been reasonably successful as the Bewleys had the biggest house in town and the first television set in the area.

"Mrs. Bewley, can we come in and watch the television?" was a frequent query at the Bewleys' front door.

"We're eating supper now, but come back later," she would say. I and all the other kids in town gathered in the Bewleys' living room to watch a small black and white screen with a jerky, snowy picture of the wrestling matches that emanated from station KDKA in Pittsburgh. On Saturday mornings there were Tom and Jerry cartoons, equally difficult to discern through the snow on the tiny screen.

In addition to the post office, the store had a bench out front where the men of the town and from surrounding farms would gather on summer evenings to tell lies and dirty stories and to tease us kids if we ventured too close. In the winter there was a potbellied stove at the back end of the store where the same characters congregated and told more stories. The stove put out a lot of heat and you wouldn't be there long before you shed your coat. One had to be a little careful not to get in the line of fire of the tobacco juice spitters. The sizzle of the stove when the spittle missives hit the side of the stove was rather impressive. The store was open for business during those evenings but not much commerce took place except for the occasional bottle of pop or the purchase of a slice of bologna and two saltine crackers that went for a nickel. The mustard that went on the bologna was free.

Further nicknames were bestowed on the Rinehart boys, Richard aka Damel and Guy aka Mousy. Their father was an over-the-road truck driver and was seldom seen but his wife, Rosie, was very much in evidence. They lived in a large house at the other end of the town. They also had a barn and a field where they kept a couple cows. We got our milk from them and, despite the milk bypassing the pasteurization process, we never got either brucellosis or tuberculosi. Knowing the temperament of Damel and Mousy, I wouldn't be surprised that some adulteration of the milk took place from time to time, and they definitely took the cream off the top before bringing the milk pail to our house, as the milk was rather blue. Thus I have been drinking skim milk all of my life.

There were a couple of girls in our town who were a bit slow and were known respectively as Gooseneck and Gaspipe. We thought that because of their intellect that they might be seducible, but they weren't that dumb. Perhaps one of the cruelest nicknames was bestowed on my good friend Neil Hagan, whom we all called Stink. I think it arose from his use of Brilliantine on his hair that, in addition to its red color, had a pronounced sweet fragrance. Roger Ackerman was known as Dutch, referring to a slight speech impediment. He would refer to his sister, Lois, as Seestor, and so I sometimes greet my sister Margaret Jean as Seestor to this day. Their cousin Clarence was known as Boozer. A guy named Bill Hagan was always referred to as Willy Lump Lump, and his uncle was called Hagie, although I'm sure he had a real name. Brother David, sometime in his grade school years, was in love with a girl named Donna Hannah, known to all of us as Fireball. Other notable alternate names included Willis "Pewee" Yarnall, Richard

"Butch" Carpenter, Junior Burga, Marvin Chef Boy ar Dee Steed, Jack Plumly and his son Derwin "Derv" Plumly. A couple of other Manns were known as Rocky or Whiskey. Then there was Ducky Warfield, Bob "Lollipop" Lallathin and especially Lela "Battleax" Mahoney, our third- and fourth-grade teacher. This being the age of corporal punishment in schools as well as at home, she administered a couple of whippings on me. I remember the reasons, appropriate as they were, but we'll skip those details.

Clayton Rogers, whose nickname I have forgotten, had a small hardware store, but he earned his living largely by doing plumbing and other types of handyman chores around town. The constant chatter that he provided didn't seem to slow him up much from his tasks. He had four sons, only one of whom had a nickname to my knowledge (Eugene=CB Westerns). Sadly, the oldest, Clarence, was an early casualty of World War II, one of two deaths from our area although there were many young men serving in various parts of the world during the war similar to what I have described for Francis Brock. Thus, although several houses in Somerton displayed red, white and blue banners in their windows indicating that a member of the family was serving in the armed services, the Rogers' window was the only one that displayed a Gold Star indicative of the sacrifice of their son. Clayton was a bit of a BS'er, and he frequently told the story of how he had saved his high school basketball team from defeat. I suspect that this occurred not too long after the peach baskets were replaced by metal hoops and nylon nets. Apparently Clayton was ill and didn't dress for the game but was in attendance, sitting in the crowd. At halftime his team was down 6 to 4 and things looked bleak until his coach called him out of the crowd and said, "Clayton, dress." Naturally, Clayton entered the game in the second half and sunk two long-range set shots to win the game. The story must have been true as I heard him repeat it more than once.

World War II

TELEPHONE EQUIPMENT IN OUR AREA was a wooden, wall-mounted box with a crank and a dial, a speaker and a receiver. Everyone who subscribed to the phone service had this type of a phone. They were all connected to one another, so we were on a party line. All conversations were for all and intents and purposes in the public domain. Because every household had a distinctive telephone ring — ours was one long and two shorts — the identity of the parties was also known. Calls in the middle of the night were infrequent enough that if there was one you could be sure the news, glad or sad, would be shared. Garfield Butcher — yes that was his name — owned and operated the telephone service and one night late the phone rang a few times before Garfield got out of bed and opened up the switchboard. "Rosie, who are you trying to call at this time of night?" "I'm trying to call my son who is in the Air Force in England. You know it's morning time over there now. The number is Bluffington 26." Garfield was having trouble understanding and Rosie Rinehart kept repeating, "Bluffington, Bluffington." When Garfield said, "You mean B as in bullshit?" Daddy practically fell to the floor laughing!

During the war, we 7-, 8-, 9- and 10-year-old boys didn't play much cowboys and Indians. Instead, we played war — crawling around in the weeds with sticks for a gun and "killing" each other as we assumed the roles of the Japs or the Germans. We also aided the war effort by collecting milkweed pods, which we were told were used to stuff life vests for pilots, as well as zinc jar lids, pieces of rubber and I don't know what else. We were taught how to identify the silhouette of enemy warplanes and to be on the lookout for any spies. One time a young man walked into town carrying a guitar and a small duffle bag. He looked as American as the rest of us, but there was some concern as to why he wasn't in uniform. He had noticed the tobacco packinghouse and asked if it would be all right if he slept there for the night. It was OK with the men of the town who made such decisions but as twilight began to fall, suspicions of his being a spy began to murmur through the crowd sitting in front of Bewley's store. This became a posse that escorted him out of town. Somerton had an organized Civilian Defense Corps who met occasionally and discussed strategy. I can't imagine what the strategy was and I don't know exactly what Daddy's official position was, but he had a big white metal helmet and a whistle that he kept at the ready.

When the servicemen returned home, either on furlough or after being discharged, we kids pestered them incessantly to give us some of their shoulder patches and insignia. Several of them had Purple Heart medals and other awards that they weren't going to give up, but by the time the war ended I had a box full of armed service memorabilia. The Byers family had three flags in their window indicating the three boys who were older than my pals who were in the service. A couple of men brought back more permanent souvenirs, such as the glass eye that my friend Neil Hagan's father, Harvey, acquired. There were also a few "war brides," the most notable being the beautiful French girl that Neil Carpenter introduced to our little insular community.

Saints and Sinners

"Jim, can I read that new Captain Marvel comic book if you're done with it?"

"No, Dad hasn't read it yet. You can have it after him."

And eventually the comic book would come to me. I didn't have any money to spend on comic books or much of anything else, but Jim loaned me things and we frequently relied on him for transportation when he got old enough to drive. In contrast to some of us, Jim and his brother Chud were somewhat privileged children, and they had plenty of toys and footballs and basketballs and ball gloves that they shared with us more or less freely. The Gibbons family lived above the grocery store, which gave Jim access to all the candy he wanted and caused his teeth to rot out at a very early age. It made sense that Jim and I would grow up together, as we lived just across the street from the store. Fat Robert was a little more lenient about extending credit to us than were the Bewleys who ran the other store, and it was certainly easier for one of us the run across the street for a bottle of milk or a loaf of bread and tell either Fat Robert, his wife, Evelyn, or Grandpa Jess, Grandma Lena or whoever was minding the store at the moment to "Put it on the bill." Jim could always be relied on to go somewhere with me or to drive my mother to Barnesville to see the doctor or whatever.

He was a saint in that regard, although his personal behavior wouldn't always suggest that and he got into as much mischief as any of the rest of us. He was an excellent tenor saxophone player and started playing dance gigs when he was a freshman in high school. He even worked a few years as a professional musician but eventually he got tired of smoking cigarettes, drinking cheap gin and chasing women who, incidentally, were always falling over him, He became a Methodist minister. Years later he even preached my mother's funeral service.

I describe him as a saint in contrast to Norman Carter, who spent a sizeable segment of his adult life in the Ohio State Penitentiary. Norman was my age and we went through school together including the transfer to Barnesville for the senior year. He lived with his brother Virgil and his Dad, without a mother, on a small farm in an outlying area known as Flatrock. Another small settlement that was also served by the Somerton schools school bus was called Stumptown. This did resemble a town with a couple of houses and a small church where services were held perhaps every other Sunday. The preacher of the Methodist church in Somerton was responsible for two or three of these outlying churches. Norman was a reasonable guy and I actually spent a couple of nights out at Flatrock at their house. A cousin from Chicago, Augie, came to live with them for a few months and he was rough character, but it was a good introduction to people who might be a bit more worldly and aggressive than we were used to. Norman ultimately got a job as a school custodian after we graduated high school and over the course of a few years he went to school part time and was able to change careers to that of a grade school teacher. Not long after graduating from high school, he married a girl named Sally Kennard — the Kennard of the M & K Grocery Company where my father worked. Although there wasn't much delineation of social status in the area, there was enough to cause concern that Sally had lowered herself to marry Norman. Apparently Norman wasn't a very faithful husband and had a few girlfriends on the side. This particular appetite was his undoing. He became involved with a young girl and at one point he beat her up so badly that she filed assault charges against him. Fearing that if the case came to trial and made the newspapers, he would lose his job as a teacher, he made plans to prevent the girl from testifying against him by buying a handgun and hiring a local thug to kill her. Somehow the plot became known, and Norman was ultimately convicted of conspiracy and death threats and spent several years at the Graybar Hotel in Columbus.

Mischief, Misdemeanors and Felonies

JOHN BATES WAS SITTING IN HIS LIVING ROOM one October evening reading the Martins Ferry Times Leader that I had delivered to him earlier in the day when a sudden loud and ratcheting noise jolted him out of his chair. "What the hell was that?" Seeing nothing out the window or from the front door he had resumed his reading when the sound appeared again. Again, nothing could be discerned from looking outside, but the sound was really rather familiar to several houses in Somerton, this being Halloween time. There was no such thing as trick or treat in those days — it was all trick. The rasping sound was produced by making notches in a wooden spool of sewing thread. placing a stick for an axle in the center of the spool, and then winding the spool with a length of strong string — probably stolen from Gibbons' store. When the spool was placed on a windowpane, the axle held, and the string pulled to rotate the notched spool, creating a fearful noise that reverberated through the victim's house. Of course, after we had annoyed the occupants of the house a few times and had not been caught, we finished that part of the evening by covering the windows with soap, ensuring that the homeowner would have some cleaning to do in the coming days. We also did a lot of annoying things like ringing the doorbell or knocking on the door and running away or unleashing someone's dog. The time we threw a box of burning leaves into an old lady's house probably counts as a felony rather than a misdemeanor. Some of the older boys liked to tip over outhouses. The story that someone was sitting in the outhouse when it was tipped over was a recurring small-town legend. If it's true, that sort of assault on a person takes it out of the dirty tricks or misdemeanor category. Another activity of the older boys was cow tipping. This was the province of the older boys, as it requires a fair bit of cooperative strength to tip over a reluctant several-hundred-pound bovine.

One of our favorite daytime stunts was what we called the "pocketbook trick." At the top of the hill at the edge of town was a fairly long flat stretch of the highway with a deep ditch on either side where we performed this ritual. The trick consisted of getting an old pocketbook, tying a sturdy string to it and laying it in the middle of the road with the urchins holding on to the other end of the string while crouching in the ditch out of sight of the motorist. Seeing the purse lying in the road ready to be claimed caused many a motorist to stop suddenly and back up to retrieve the bounty but, of course, while he was backing up his car we reeled in the string and the purse and ran off further into the bushes. The thought that this trick might result in an accident never entered our minds. We relished the astonished look on the driver's face when he discovered he had been sucked in by a mirage. The highway was not only a link to the outer world, but it also was our playground and figured into a couple of other dangerous misdemeanors.

It was a dark and stormy night. It really was and it seemed like a good time to climb up into the large sycamore tree that hung out over the road in front of the Rineharts' house and drop water-filled balloons onto passing cars. The cars weren't going very fast, having just labored up the long hill at the south end of town. One unsuspecting traveler was a man by the name of Tommy Skinner who lived a couple miles north of town and who was a frequent visitor to the Corner Grill in Malaga. When the balloon hit his windshield, he was sober enough to stop the car immediately, jump out and chase us around the back of the house as we clambered out of the tree. As we all crowded into the back door, I being the smallest of the group was left in the grasp of an irate, drunk Tommy. Just as he was about to send me to Never Never Land with his fist a couple of the older guys grabbed him and calmed him down a bit before putting him in his old Ford and watching him wobble up the road. It took me a bit longer to calm down as I realized he could have really done me serious damage.

A similar fortuitous arrangement of a tree over the road happened to be in front of Earl and Edna Doudna's house in the center of town. One summer evening Damel Rinehart climbed the tree with a supply of water balloons and proceeded to christen cars as they came by. One driver didn't see the fun in this activity, stopped his car and ran back under the tree, where he spotted Damel. In other words Damel was "treed" much as one might tree a raccoon on a winter night with the help of blue tick hounds. Ever resourceful, Damel climbed out on a large limb and onto the porch roof of the house, all the while mindful of the man on the ground yelling and shaking his fist at him. Since it was summer, the Doudnas kept their windows open, so Damel simply went into their bedroom, crept past the sleeping old couple and down to the first floor where he exited through the back door and ran away. The car driver never caught him and the homeowners never knew he had been in their bedroom.

It seems like more than one of my misadventures involved heights. The packinghouses at the back of the town were huge with several stories of large beams set at a distance apart to accommodate tobacco sticks that were spaced between the beams and allowed the large leaves of tobacco to hang and dry. There was a large supply of these tobacco sticks stored in the old packinghouse, and they were very useful as a hiking aid, a club, a hobbyhorse, a pretend sword or a musket. Whatever kind of wood those sticks were made of, they were very sturdy. I'm not sure what I was looking for one day when I climbed to the top row of beams, but no sooner had I reached my goal than I looked down to the ground floor and saw a man walking slowly through the building carrying a rifle. Whether he was shooting rats or pigeons or whatever, I thought it best to hold my breath and not move lest he might shoot at any little movement he detected in the building. After he left, I cautiously climbed down and didn't look back as I ran to the house.

Another place we liked to mess around in was an abandoned coal mine outside of town. A rock or a pebble tossed into an abandoned mine shaft seems to take a couple of seconds before it reaches the surface of the water which, over the years, has filled the shaft. The impact creates a sharp, tinkling sound and then an echo. It's too dark to see the expanding, circular wavelets on the water's surface that are certainly there. If we had fallen into the shaft, we would have made a similar but larger splash and it's really a miracle that we didn't fall in as we climbed around on the rickety old tipple — a sort of tower that was erected over the mine and supported the rude elevator that one rode to descend into the mine and the trams loaded with coal that were hauled to the surface and tipped over to unload. Hence the name apparently. The other dangerous part about playing around the mine was, boys being boys, we were always pushing each other and grabbing each other, threatening to throw one into the black hole. If that had happened there would be no rescue.

We seemed to do a fair bit of breaking and entering. There were a couple unoccupied houses or sheds, one of which was said to be owned by a deputy sheriff but he was never around and the house contained all sorts of treasures. Perhaps a better source of "stuff" was a fairly large shed down toward the middle of town that contained all sorts of small machines, tools and implements of the mining trade.

Garfield Butcher of the "English telephone caper" died shortly after that episode and his widow remained in the small brick house at the edge of town. This house was allegedly a station on the Underground Railroad and thus a source of immense curiosity for young boys. We would sneak in the back door and rummage around the storage rooms looking for evidence of the slave passages but never really found anything and never alerted Mrs. Butcher to the point of us getting caught or scaring the hell out of her.

From Boyhood to Adulthood

I HAVE TRIED TO CONFINE THIS TALE to my boyhood, but some incidents from high school have crept in. I specifically don't want to chronicle my high school years though. Suffice it to say that high school is high school with its trials and triumphs, and I can't imagine that my experiences are that much different from other kids that would make for very interesting reading.

When barely 18 years old, on a night that is cold and windy, I stood tiredly on 16th Street in Washington, D.C., waiting for the Georgia Avenue bus. My Uncle Charles had come to Barnesville for my high school graduation and, as I had no plans and no prospects, he took me back to Silver Spring and helped me get a job in a bank where his wife, Mary, worked. Uncle Robert and Aunt Libby had a spare bedroom that they rented to me for $13 a month. When September rolled around, I enrolled as a part-time student at American University and traveled into D.C. a couple evenings a week for my classes. I didn't adapt to college very well and didn't particularly like my job at the bank and I really didn't like my boss so that cold and windy evening was the pivot point that sent me back to Appalachia. Truth be told, I was also homesick. It didn't take me long to move to Warren, Ohio, and move in with my friend Stink Hagan at his grandmother's house. I got a very boring job at a General Motors plant, sitting at a machine and watching a huge spool of insulated copper wire disappear into baskets full of wires of varying lengths. I would periodically grab a bundle of wires and dip the ends into a pot of molten lead that would splatter and inflict small burns on my hands and arms. That job convinced me that I had better get a better ticket and as soon as I had saved enough money, I was off to college on a full-time basis.

I guess I was still a boy when I went off to college, but I'm not going to touch that period of my life either. Somehow, I managed to do well enough in the classroom in 3½ years to gain admission to medical school despite a lot of college-age mischief and misdemeanors that are probably best forgotten.

Made in the USA
Columbia, SC
22 November 2024

47330389R00045